Loved in God's Heart

Devotions for Foster Children and Orphans

Teresa Ann Winton

Scripture taken from:
NEW AMERICAN STANDARD BIBLE®,
Copyright © 1960,1962,1963,1968,1971,1972,1973,1975,1977,1995
by The Lockman Foundation. Used by permission.
ESV® Bible (The Holy Bible, English Standard Version®), copyright © 2001 by Crossway, a publishing ministry of Good News Publishers. Used by permission. All rights reserved.
Holy Bible, King James Version, Cambridge 1769. Public domain.

ISBN: 978-1-7344627-2-2

Cover design and illustrations by Valentina Burimenko
Interior design and layout by Ian Winton
Editing by Ian Winton
Author photograph by Craft Photographic Gallery

Dedication

A few years ago I shared excerpts from my personal journal entries with some of my close friends. They expressed they had been inspired and urged me to publish the collection of diaries. With much prayer, I decided my friends were right; I had to step out and be God's pen for others who have also suffered the wounds of rejection.

Loved in the Locket of God's Heart is a collection of memoir pieces that inspired my relationship with God. The pearls of wisdom revealed in this book have taken most my of life to discover. If I had had a condensed book like this when I was first taken into foster care, I may have been spared greater hurt and confusion.

I dedicate this book to you, Ian, my cherished son.

I also dedicate this book to Ricky, Rachael, Tim, Charlotte, Freddie, and the memory of Tracy.

Foster child, orphan, homeless, and anyone who needs a place to belong, this book is for you. I hope you will find, through my personal journey, an emotional and spiritual guide to coming home to God.

"There is hope for your future," declares the Lord.
—Jeremiah 31:17

Acknowledgments

First and foremost, I'd like to thank God—my forever family—who lifted me out of great suffering and showered me with blessings, compassion, and love. I thank Him for giving me the gift of determination that has allowed me to persevere through loss and hardship. I praise Him for helping me to find pearls of wisdom born out the painful experiences that have provided insight in writing these devotions.

An appreciation also goes to Ian, for your careful editing and beautiful formatting of this book. The journey to bringing this book to life is special and I will always cherish the time we've had together. I love you!

My beloved siblings; I appreciate you being my dear family and supporting my writing through the years.

Thank you, my friends—those in the past and those in the present—for seeing my value and helping me to find the good things inside myself. You are dear and I count you as family!

Thank you to the many spiritual teachers and mentors who have guided me over the years. A special thanks goes to you, Greg, for supporting and advising me on deeper Biblical truths contained in this book. Thank you also for proofreading my manuscript.

I wish to acknowledge the following for all their words of encouragement and prayers during the creation of this book: Patricia, Laurie, Ruth, John & Brenda, Dan, Dennis & Linda, Marshall & Glenda, Tim, Laurene & Hubert, Norman, Teresa, my friends at Central and Cherokee Church, and my Facebook friends.

Thank you, Valentina, for the outstanding work you've done on this book! I was delighted when we reconnected and were able to work together again. I love the designs! Thank you!

I also want to thank Shirley for encouraging me to journal as a method of therapy during my painful youth. You were an inspiration to many, especially to me. Thank you!

Thank you, my wonderful fans, for buying my books and remaining loyal readers.

Table of Contents

God Whispers Hope

All Scripture is breathed out by God.
—2 Timothy 3:16

Sometimes the most innocent and vulnerable among us suffer the greatest in this world. You've suffered a broken heart and a fallen world, and are now in foster care or an orphanage. Even though today you cannot fathom how God's going to use these tragic circumstances for your good or how He'll make a way for you to survive, be assured He will. The Lord holds you close to His heart; He will carry you when the pain is more than you can bear.

As you search for normalcy after losing your family, you can become overwhelmed with sorrow and even feel small under its boulder of pain. Remember, you are not small nor are you alone; your troubles do not define or limit you. You have an eternal Father whose heart is unsearchable and whose resources are inexhaustible.

No matter how dark your circumstances or how insignificant you may feel, the light of God's love surrounds all areas of your life; in Him there is an ever-glowing candle to illuminate your path.

God is the author and finisher of our faith when we choose to honor and obey him. Honoring God is how we find a relationship with Him and ultimately restoration of our broken lives. With God as our foundation, we can have a good ending, despite having a tragic beginning. We don't have to live as shattered orphans who have no hope. We are God's children with a place to belong in the locket of His heart.

God's word is a fortress, our castle where we can find peace, love, hope, healing, inspiration, and forgiveness. Any time, night or day, in the highs and in the lows of life, God is available. He longs to hear everything on our heart.

In this book I'll share Scriptures, poems, and songs that have helped me survive and heal from the devastating wounds of having been a child of the foster care system. I'll also share personal experiences that may in some way affirm you are not alone in how you feel or in the journey toward wholeness. I hope as you begin to read this book, you'll be inspired to get a Bible of your own so that you'll be enriched in the breath of God.

Also included in this devotion are illustrated pages on which you can pen your personal thoughts, prayers, poems, hopes, dreams, and artwork. This book is yours to express whatever you wish and how you wish to express it. Perhaps you would want to keep it in your backpack or purse so that it's always with you as a source of comfort.

It is my prayer that as you begin to read and express yourself on the extra pages, you will keep in the forefront of your mind that God knows how you feel and is there to help you. You can be assured that even though you may feel abandoned without a mother and father, God sees you differently.

In John 14:18, Jesus says, "I *have not left you as orphans; I will come to you.*" You have the Holy Spirit there with you for comfort, as well as the entire host of Heaven looking out for you. Embrace God's heart and He'll light the path for you to find a father, mother, an eternal family that will never leave or disappoint.

Today is your new beginning to great peace, joy, and strength. Go to your secret place with the Lord; He waits with open arms to comfort, inspire, and give you renewed hope. Make His word the first thing you see when you open your eyes in the morning and the last thing you focus on before falling asleep, and you will find amazing strength and peace. His serene presence will quiet the raging waters within your soul, soothing you through the scary, uncertain times. God loves you and will bless you with a forever home in His Heart; His breath whispers hope over you today!

Fill your paper with the breathings of your heart.
–William Wordsworth

Dear lord Please forgive me
for running away from my Pain.
Please understand how I feel. I
thank you so dearly for helping
me find Julia, you told me to
Pick her I Know it. Lord I
believe that me and you have
a strong bond. I Pray you
tell me what I should do next,
lord what do you have Planed
for me. I love you
dearly — your child.

Three Stands of Love

*A cord of three strands
is not quickly torn apart.*
−Ecclesiastes 4:12

In the heart of God there is peace, hope, love, and affection. When life gets tough and you feel you cannot hold on a moment longer, cling to God's Word, the Holy Spirit, and Jesus and you'll find an anchor to hold onto.

The Bible is where you will find three strands of family love. The Scriptures will be a source of wisdom and a guide to understanding God. The Holy Spirit is where you'll find comfort. Jesus will be your mediator, savior, and friend.

Your troubles may not be solved immediately in doing this, but holding on to God gives you peace while you await rescue. Having someone there is enough sometimes to get us through a dark, lonely time. There is no greater place for comfort and peace than in the loving, all-encompassing heart of God.

Fill your paper with the breathings of your heart.
– William Wordsworth

Eternal Fingerprints

Set me as a seal upon thine heart,
as a seal upon thine arm:
for love is strong as death.
—Song of Songs 8:6

Y ou belong to God and are never-ending with Him. His love and devotion are timeless; He never loses interest in you or prefers another over you. You are always on His mind and remembered as He ponders ways to make you happy, keep you safe, and repair the shattered places in your heart.

Ephesians 1:5 reads: *He predestined us to adoption as sons through Jesus Christ to Himself, according to the kind intention of His will.* I remember when someone read this Scripture to me and told me I was God's adopted daughter and nothing or no one would destroy His great love for me. And so it is with you: you are God's child and belong to Him! Notice the words of the previous Scripture; *according to the kind intention of His will.* God is thoughtfully kind toward you!

Our earthly families are temporary. Whether we have an earthly family or not, none of it will exist in the afterlife. The Scripture above affirms we're all adopted. While earthly families are important and essential to our well being, they do not compare to the joyful family waiting for us in Heaven.

Whenever you feel unloved or forgotten, remember you are the Father's dearest love, His little girl! You are His masterpiece; designed as a part of His eternal fingerprint with family whose never going to hurt, disappoint, or leave.

Fill your paper with the breathings of your heart.
— William Wordsworth

After this reading I felt grateful that my Parents are still alive and that I get to talk to them on the Phone. I Know god is there for me, but Sometimes it feels as if he doesnt listen to my Prayers because he doesnt answer them. For example I have asked and Prayed for my mom to get better and

She is in Prison. I have also Prayed for a better home but that has not been answered either.

Forever Father

W hen you've become a ward of the state or do not know your family roots you may feel the need to search for your family tree. The pursuit could leave you with more heartaches and questions than you had before.

Foster children and orphans are often not afforded the luxury of having a scrapbook of their childhood. Sometimes the only items they have are clothes they're wearing when removed from their home. The night I was taken from my parents, I held onto my mother's skirt, but even that was torn from me when I was whisked away.

In one of the homes where I lived there was a large family Bible displayed on the coffee table. One day I opened the book and began reading the inside cover taking notice of the marriages, births, and family death records. I sat pondering the names of the people and how special they must have been to have their names recorded inside the pages of a Bible.

My thoughts then took me to the realization that my name or my family's names weren't written in the book. I left the room feeling rejected and unloved. I was further upset when the social worker had told me this was my new family where I'd be loved and accepted. "So why weren't my family's names listed in the Bible too?" I thought.

If you're lacking a scrapbook of your childhood, remember God has kept a memory book of you. He has recorded every hurt, every triumph, and every detail about you, filling each page as you've lived every moment.

Psalm 139:16 reads: *Your eyes have seen my unformed substance; And in Your book were all written the days that were ordained for me, when as yet there was not one of them.* This scripture reveals powerful details about all of us! We were not a casual thought on God's heart; we were cherished and considered before our mothers gave birth to us!

God is your all-knowing architect. In secret, He planned you and sketched you in His book before you were born. He recorded your days on His scroll, designing the blueprint of your being for His divine purposes. He knows you inside and out and He knows the beauty within you. He loved you before you were born!

The next time you feel sad because you don't have a family photo or any tangible memento of your former life, remember the Lord's observation of you is intentional. He wrote about you before there was something to write about. No one in the world can ever love you with the intensity of God's love and devotion. He's your forever Father. You're name is on God's family tree; there you will never be forgotten or cast aside.

Fill your paper with the breathings of your heart.
-William Wordsworth

Held as God's Children

Through the years I have deeply missed not having a dad to talk with. The years that were stolen have left me tearfully wishing my father had been there sharing my dreams, helping with my problems, and loving me as his little girl. I've envisioned sitting and sipping coffee with my dad on many occasions and imagining his smile as he sat listening and cherishing me.

Not having our parents alongside us as we grow, can leave us vulnerable with an insatiable need to be loved and validated. But only God can truly fill the emptiness in our souls. He wants to be our main source for love. Unlike our friends and family members, God has an unlimited supply of time, love, and wisdom to give. It's healthy and right to lean on friends for love and support, but keeping a healthy balance of our expectations of them is worth considering.

Isaiah 66:13 reads: "As one whom his mother comforts, so I will comfort you; And you will be comforted in Jerusalem." This Scripture portrays God with the same emotions and desires as a loving mother whose heart yearns deeply and compassionately for her children. There is no greater depth of comfort to be found anywhere than in the all-consuming arms of God. He will pursue you to all ends the earth if that's what it takes to bring you into His love, protection, and comfort!

1 John 3:1 reads: *See what kind of love the Father has given to us, that we should be called children of God; and so we are.* This verse is proof that God regards us as His little children, love He freely bestowed on us. Not only is God our Father and we His children, but His love and devotion are never-ending.

When you're forced to live without your parents and miss their touch or hearing them tell you they love you, close your eyes and try to imagine God holding you in His lap. Have a child-like trust in Him, expressing all of your fears, sorrows, and disappointments. Empty out the entire contents of your heart to Him because He cares so deeply for you.

His Love endures forever.
—Psalm 136

Fill your paper with the breathings of your heart.
– William Wordsworth

Unforgettable

"Can a woman forget her nursing child and have no compassion on the son of her womb? Even these may forget, but I will not forget you. Behold, I have inscribed you on the palms of My hands; Your walls are continually before Me."
—Isaiah 49:15-16

his image is a beautiful expression of grace and elegance, and is expressed as a maternal regard that God has for His people. The love God has for you is stronger than that which is produced by the most tender, earthly ties.

The love of a mother for her infant child is the strongest attachment in nature and most mothers would not refuse or turn their backs on their children. It may be hard to believe our mothers consider us after we've been taken from them or that they ever really wanted us after rights were terminated. But I have known of mothers who spent all of their lives wanting to be near their child, but the child never gave them the chance to be forgiven or the opportunity to show them a changed heart.

Perhaps we cannot go back and be little children again in our mother's arms, but we can rebuild from where we are. As painful as it is, we must first forgive those who have hurt us and then allow God to do what we cannot.

But Jesus looked at them and said, "With man this is impossible, but with God all things are possible."
—Matthew 19:26

If your mother isn't in your life remember God's love for you is deeper than all earthly, maternal feelings. His love is forever; He never lets go! You are always in God's sight and dear to His heart. In fact, so dear, that He has engraved you on His hand as a way to keep you with Him always!

Fill your paper with the breathings of your heart.
– William Wordsworth

Home in God's Heart

A Prayer of Moses, the man of God, is recorded in Psalm 90. Moses never had a true home. His mother hid him at birth to protect him from being killed by Pharaoh. He was eventually raised by one of Pharaoh's daughters.

It's recorded in Deuteronomy 34 that when Moses died, the Lord buried him, and to this day, no one knows where his grave is. There's something very significant and touching about the story of Moses. To know God loved His child so much that He buried him and has not allowed anyone to know the location of his burial is poignant and beautiful. Even though Moses did not have a connected blood family, he had the best home of all, God's heart!

Psalm 84 tells of the bird having a home, the swallow a nest for herself so that she may have her young. If God takes into account every detail of His creatures and cared for Moses with honor and respect, He most certainly considers you and your well-being.

The word *home* is mentioned fifty-one times in the King James Bible. It's evident God places a great deal of importance to providing homes for all of His creation. Ephesians 2:19 reads: *So then you are no longer* strangers and aliens, but you are fellow citizens with the saints, and are of God's household. All believers are considered God's children, having complete access to the temple of God, His house. This is a comforting thought for those of us who never had a permanent place to call home. The next time you see a bird with her young, remember God has already made a home for you in His heart. Accept God's love and allow Him to console you.

God has made a home
in the heavens for the sun.
—Psalm 19:4

Fill your paper with the breathings of your heart.
—William Wordsworth

Apple of God's Eye

He found him in a desert land, and in the howling
waste of a wilderness; He encircled him, He cared for
him, He guarded him as the pupil of His eye.
—Deuteronomy 32:10

Y ou are God's beloved. He is circled around you, guarding and constantly watching over you day and night. He will keep your soul safe and protected from all evil and from every enemy.

God wishes to gather us—his children—under His wings to protect us. *How often I wanted to gather your children together, the way a hen gathers her chicks under her wings* (Matthew 23:37). This is a tender image of God's affection for us.

Nature is one of the best places to find poetic expressions of God's love for us. Consider the mother hen, for example, she is on guard at all times watching for approaching danger. As soon as the lives of her babies are threatened, she swoops over and gathers them under her wings for protection.

Psalm 139:17-18 reads: *How precious also are your thoughts of me, O God! How vast is the sum of them! If I should count them they would outnumber the sand. You* are of great value to God. He holds you close to His heart, and like the sands on the seashore, His thoughts of you are endless. Through all seasons He remains unchanged; a circle that cannot be broken.

From everlasting to everlasting, thou art God.
—Psalm 90:1

It's impossible for anyone, including the most loving earthly parents, to supersede God's tender, watchful care of you. We owe Him everything because He's been with us through every experience—disappointment, sorrow, and defeat—giving us all that we have.

He shall cover thee with His feathers,
and under His wings shalt thou trust:
His truth shall be thy shield and buckler.
—Psalm 91:4

Fill your paper with the breathings of your heart.
–William Wordsworth

Held in God's Hand

I give eternal life to them,
and they will never perish;
and no one will
snatch them out of My hand.
—John 10:28

God promises to hold you in the hollow of His hand. That will never change despite how you may feel about yourself or how others think of you. God pursues you as if you are the only one in the world. He surrounds you: He's behind you, in front of you, and and on all sides, guarding and protecting you. No force can tear you away from His mighty hand!

You have enclosed me
behind and before,
and laid Your hand upon me.
—Psalm 139:5

2 Chronicles 16:9 reads: *For the eyes of the Lord run to and fro throughout the whole earth, to shew himself strong in the behalf of them whose heart is perfect toward him.* This is a small verse, but it speaks volumes about God's presence; somehow the world doesn't

seem so big and troubles as consuming when the eyes of Eternity are overseeing us.

It takes courage to step into the unknown after losing everything you once knew. There will be times when you will be in a room or place all alone without comfort. Or you may find as I once did, you get off the school bus, a state car is parked in your driveway; your bags are packed and you're told you're moving to another home.

But you don't have to be afraid or feel alone because God is there keeping His eye on you. You are under His constant care and abiding protection! If you're feeling alone or afraid, close your eyes and imagine God's arms around you and Jesus cupping your face in His hands and you won't feel so alone or scared.

The LORD is for me; I will not fear;
what can man do to me?
—Psalm 118:6

Fill your paper with the breathings of your heart.
–William Wordsworth

God Will Take You In

God makes a home for the lonely;
He leads out the prisoners into prosperity,
Only the rebellious dwell in a parched land.
—Psalm 68:5

For those who never knew their parents or siblings it can be difficult when they want to explore their family roots. You may ponder what features you share with other family members as you seek to find your identity.

Years ago, when I was allowed to visit with my parents and siblings, I can recall taking notice of the features we had in common. The time we shared comforted me while strengthening our family bond.

If you never knew your biological family, take note of what God says about you in the Bible. Genesis 1:27 reads: *So God created man in his own image, in the image of God created he him; male and female created he them.* You posses an immortal soul and have access to God's purity, His power, His strength, His unfailing love, and ultimately a dwelling place with Him in Heaven! All of this can be yours through the sacrifice His son, Jesus Christ, made on the cross.

If you've been abandoned, consider what God says in Psalms 27:10: "*For my father and my mother have forsaken me, but the LORD will take me in.*" You read it correctly; God will take you in. There's always an open door when God's your home! If you're living on the street or are with people who don't have your best interests at heart, seek shelter with a church in your area. At the least, pray God sends someone your way to help you find His love and direction.

God will love you no matter what you've done or where you've been. He'll supply all your needs, physical, emotional, and spiritual. There's always a way out of every trouble. Even when everyone around you has given up on you God never will! He will always welcome you back no matter what has happened. Satan seeks to try to convince you that you're not worthy of anyone's love or that you've messed up beyond repair. Those are lies; don't listen to him!

If you are struggling to find your identity, remember you belong to royalty, an eternal lineage shared with Deity. The family jewels await you when you choose to love, obey, and honor God. He supplies our need for a father, mother, family, and Creator. Beautiful daughter of God, build your hopes and dreams on the isle of Eternity where God waits to place a crown on your head.

Hearts unfold like flowers before Thee,
opening to the sun above. Melt the clouds of sin and
sadness; drive the dark of doubt away.
—Ludwig Van Beethoven

Fill your paper with the breathings of your heart.
                    —William Wordsworth

Jesus Wept

J ohn 11:35 reads: *Jesus wept.* This is known as the shortest verse in the Bible. Those two words carry an enormous weight, however. This was the first Bible verse I clung to as solace when I was in foster care. I recall lying on my bed late one evening and tears pouring as I read this powerful Scripture; as the tears fell, I wailed while caressing the verse with my hand.

I read the verse over and over, thinking of Jesus crying like I did. Somehow, knowing the Lord also felt sad helped me not to feel alone. It was as if I had made a new friend who understood me, who cried with me.

I later learned that the reason Jesus wept was over the death of his friend Lazarus. He was also moved to compassion for the others who had loved Lazarus. I believe Jesus could see into eternity in both directions: those who stood by the graves of their friends and families and those who would do so in the future. Perhaps this is why Jesus was moved to tears when He knew He had the power to raise Lazarus to life.

The next time you cry or feel alone, revisit this powerfully touching story and be comforted as I once was. Or write down a Scripture that helps you feel understood. If you don't have a Scripture in mind, open your Bible and pray for God to reveal one to you and He will!

We find in Isaiah 53:3 that Jesus was despised, rejected, and acquainted with grief. He is your Savior who understands and has felt the deep wounds like those inside your soul. He was tender, compassionate, and kind toward all, and yet many sought to trick, blaspheme, and put Him to death for sins He never committed.

Trust Jesus as your Savior; He's your advocate, defender, and empathetic friend. He knows how rejection and abandonment feels and what it's like to suffer as an innocent man. There's tremendous reassurance and comfort to be found in meditating on the life of Jesus.

Even when one sparrow falls, God cares.
—Matthew 10:29

Fill your paper with the breathings of your heart.
 – William Wordsworth

God Is Your Friend

The Lord protects the strangers;
He supports the fatherless and the widow.
—Psalm 146:9

When we trust God and obey Him we can be happy knowing He's defending and guiding the fatherless and widows. The strangers who are away from home and friends can also find sympathy because God has not forsaken them either.

Whenever you feel alone, unloved or forgotten remember the Lord loves and adores you. He is for you. Even though you could not see Him, Jesus has been with you all along. He is a friend who is ever present; like bookends, He's the beginning and end to your day.

Jesus is in the room where you wail in pain. He's holding your hand and whispering, *Blessed one, keep holding on because I'm working behind the scenes to make a new path for you.*

In John 15:15 Jesus said, "*I have called you friends.*" God is your friend and promises to be your protector. He is worthy of confidence and love. Embrace His heart, and cling to His Word for He loves you more than you can comprehend. In all seasons, He is a friend who will stay with you. May you feel God's amazing love today and every day to follow.

For, behold, I am for you,
and I will turn unto you.
—Ezekiel 36:9

Fill your paper with the breathings of your heart.
–William Wordsworth

Cradled in God's Light

My breath covers you, I adore you so;
you're cradled in my light
and safe where you sleep tonight.

Many troubles seem to grow worse at night when we can't do anything about them. We can also experience nightmares or sleepwalking, particularly if we were abused or suffered disturbing traumatic events. The long nights can leave us worried, anxiety-ridden, and in need of a hand to hold, or someone to talk with about what's troubling us.

I've found it comforting to sit on my bed and read Scriptures that affirm God's love and care over me. He promises in Zephaniah 3:17 that He will quiet us with His love. The Bible is the place to find God's reassuring love.

We are told in Psalm 34:18 that the Lord is near to those who have a broken heart. You are not suffering alone: God's there now! He promises in Isaiah 30:19 that He will hear your cry and save you.

God longs to bear all of your anxieties. Psalm 55:22 reads: *Cast your burden on the Lord, and He will sustain you; He will never permit the righteous to be moved.* God is pleading for you to place all of your burdens, sorrows, and worries on His shoulders; He promises to sustain and bear both you and all that troubles you! You can also take comfort that as long as you're righteous, trusting and believing in Him, you are safe as if you were already eternal with Him.

Isaiah 30:19 is also further reassurance that the Lord will be gracious to the voice of your prayer, hearing your distress. And He promises to answer your requests in His timing. Don't get discouraged if you don't see the answers unfolding right away.

Psalm 4:8 reads: *In peace I will both lie down and sleep; for you alone, O Lord, make me dwell in safety.* I have found it helpful to chant verses like this over and over before falling asleep. The act of shifting my attention to reassuring Scriptures rather than focusing on what's upsetting me, has helped to calm me. I've also written verses like this over and over in my journal until I'm at peace and ready for sleep. Perhaps you would also find this helpful for warding off fears and anxieties that come in the night. The Lord is your candle; lie down and rest in peace knowing He will keep you safe.

Remind yourself of the promise God has made in Psalm 46:5. It reads: *God is in the midst of her, she will not be moved; God will help her when morning dawns.* Trust and know the Lord is as close as a whisper and as gentle as a baby's sigh and that help is on its way.

Fill your paper with the breathings of your heart.
— William Wordsworth

Angel of the Lord

*The angel of the Lord encamps
around those who fear Him,
and delivers them.*
—Psalm 34:7

When we've lost our former homes, we can begin to feel the protective walls of our lives have fallen. But we can take comfort in knowing that we are surrounded by a spiritual, unseen realm. Scripture reveals that not only God, Jesus, and the Holy Spirit are with us, but so are angels.

The angel of the Lord is sent by God to protect His people. Psalm 91:11 reads: *For He will give His angels charge concerning you, to guard you in all your ways.*

Even though we may not see or know they are there, angels are in our presence and are here for our good. They are sent by God to serve His will as well as to transport blessings into our lives, encourage us, strengthen us, guide us, watch over us, protect us from danger, and to help us better glorify Him.

*Angels descending, bring from above,
echoes of mercy, whispers of love.*
—Fanny J. Crosby

Fill your paper with the breathings of your heart.
– William Wordsworth

God's Self-Help Book

During all of our lives we can become consumed with trouble and not know how to get out of it. Trying to find a solution, without clear-cut direction in dealing with a crisis, can leave us in a state of panic and worry.

Aside from prayer and finding a grounded person to talk with, the Bible is a great source of insight to help with almost any problem that can arise. The book of Proverbs is a tried and true solution for nearly every trouble under the sun.

The wounds of suffering a broken home or losing parents often run deep within the soul. We can feel abandoned, afraid, angry, lost, sad, unloved, vulnerable, and worthless. These raw emotions are completely normal and must be allowed to work themselves out before we can heal.

Reading the book of Proverbs can be a wonderful tool to help deal with the powerful emotions of rejection, anger, and loss. From reading the verses, we can learn how to apply wisdom and truth to our life. Our faith will strengthen too as we find practical solutions to everyday problems. The Lord is your shelter and tower of strength, turn to Him and He will keep you safe.

> *The name of the Lord is a strong tower:*
> *the righteous runs into it, and is safe.*
> *—Proverbs 18:10*

Fill your paper with the breathings of your heart.
—William Wordsworth

Power of Prayer

The Bible is full of examples of believers who prayed and found favor with God when He answered their prayers. One of my favorite examples is the story of King Hezekiah.

The book of Isaiah records that the devout king was told to get his house in order because he was going to die. Grieved about these revelations, Hezekiah prayed for God to give him more time to live. Because Hezekiah was faithful and earnest, God granted him fifteen more years on earth.

Not only was Hezekiah healed, but God also offered him a remarkable sign: the sun's shadow went ten steps backwards! Isaiah 38:7-8 reads: "*This shall be the sign to you from the Lord, that the Lord will do this thing that He has spoken: Behold, I will cause the shadow on the stairway, which has gone down with the sun on the stairway of Ahaz, to go back ten steps.*" *So the sun's shadow went back ten steps on the stairway on which it had gone down.*

This is a powerful story of faith and the rewards that can follow when we strive with all of our heart to please God. We may not always have our prayers answered in the way we're expecting, but we can know that God will answer them according to what is best for us.

Prayer is one of the most powerful ways to find comfort, peace, and help for our troubles. Jeremiah 33:3 reads: *Call to me and I will answer you, and will tell you great and hidden things that you have not known.* We find in this Scripture God desires for us to seek Him in prayer. He also assures we'll find greater spiritual insights, pearls of wisdom, and mysteries revealed when we do.

In 1 Thessalonians 5:17 God commands us to pray without ceasing. Does that mean we literally pray non-stop doing nothing else? No, but it does imply that we are to maintain a constant spirit of prayer. Prayer should be so ingrained in our lives that it's second nature to call on God when we are in trouble. God should also be the first person we praise and thank for the answers and the blessings that follow.

Isaiah 65:24 reads: *It will also come to pass that before they call, I will answer; while they are still speaking, I will listen.* We find in this Scripture that God is powerfully attentive to the believer's prayer! He anticipates their needs and has not waited to bless them with bountiful favor and comfort. God's benevolent love is already there to grant you providential grace and favor; you need only to obey and trust to receive!

As we develop a relationship with God, we grow to love and need Him as our most preferred confidant and loyal friend. And we can know beyond a doubt, He would never give us bad advice or hurt us in any way. He's a friend who pursues us!

Stay alert at all times with prayer. Let it be the first thing you do when trials and hurts come upon you. Talk to God before calling, texting, or emailing someone else. He's your best friend, call Him first; He's expecting your call!

Thus says the Lord, the God of your father David, I have heard your prayer, I have seen your tears; behold, I will add fifteen years to your life.
—Isaiah 38:5

Fill your paper with the breathings of your heart.
— William Wordsworth

Soothing Hope

Soft as the voice of an angel,
Breathing a lesson unheard
Hope with a gentle persuasion,
Whispers her comforting word.
—Alice Hawthorne

Panic and feelings of hysteria can arise while dealing with the aftermath of tragedy. There were times in my life when the pain was so heavy upon me, I thought it would suffocate me in my sleep; I even feared my broken heart would slip away in the night. One of the best remedies, aside from prayer and reading Scripture, is to begin chanting a favorite hymn.

The above excerpt is taken from a hymn that greatly comforted me over the years. I discovered *Whispering Hope* when I was first placed in foster care. From the moment my little ears heard the song I was captivated by it. And as I grew, the lyrics became increasingly important to me.

I can recall song leaders announcing *Whispering Hope* as a hymn on the worship schedule and feeling a sense of joy because I could once again sing along with it. And in those moments my sorrows left me as my spirit soared with peace, hope, and inspiration.

The author, Septimus Winner, composed the song under the pseudonym Alice Hawthorne. Septimus was a self-taught musician with the exception of having music lessons with Leopold Meignen around 1853. But by that time, Septimus was already established as an instrumentalist, teaching and performing with ensembles. He is widely recognized for publishing ballads known as the *Hawthorne's Ballads*.

It was said Septimus Winner never intended for *Whispering Hope* to be released as a worship song, but it graces the pages of many hymnals used in worship today. I wonder if Septimus, a child of seven, had any idea how essential and inspiring his musical gifts would be long after his death.

Today, you may find yourself needing inspiration and hope. Perhaps this would be a good time to pen the lyrics to a favorite hymn or comforting song on the pages provided in this book. Having the lyrics easily accessible when unsettled feelings wash unexpectedly over your spirit, may help soothe away panic and anxiety.

You may also choose to use the page to pen your own musical expressions. It's possible that you, like Septimus Winner, have a song destined to be heard for other's hope and God's glory! If so, get your pen and write until your spirit soars in soothing joy!

With God we shall do valiantly.
—Psalm 60:12

Fill your paper with the breathings of your heart.
– William Wordsworth

Stone of Help

In the Bible we are told that Samuel, a man of God, took a stone and set it between Mizpeh and Shen, and called the name of it Ebenezer, saying, "*Hitherto hath the LORD helped us*". Ebenezer literally means "stone of help." The stone was a memorial of God's help and a reminder of what they were capable of when God was allowed to act on their behalf.

Samuel urged the house of Israel to return to the Lord with all their heart, putting away the foreign gods and the Ashtaroth from among them. He reassured the people that he would pray for them and God would deliver them. Then the people gathered at Mizpah and there they fasted and repented of their sins.

When the Philistines heard about the people of Israel gathering at Mizpah they rose up against them in battle. But the Lord thundered with a great thunder against the Philistines, confusing them, so that they were routed before Israel and then defeated. The victory belonged to the Lord and the people were helped.

We can't handle the problems and challenges of life alone; we need God's help for an optimal outcome. Just as God helped Samuel, so will He do for you! In

Psalm 46:1 we are told that He is our refuge and strength, a very present help in trouble. God is your stone of help, your cornerstone to rebuild your life on.

> *Therefore thus says the Lord God,*
> *"Behold, I am laying in Zion a stone,*
> *a tested stone, A costly cornerstone*
> *for the foundation, firmly placed.*
> *He who believes in it will not be disturbed."*
> *—Isaiah 28:16*

Fill your paper with the breathings of your heart.
–William Wordsworth

Father of Light

The unfolding of Your words gives light.
—Psalm 119:130

F ear is one of the most powerful weapons Satan uses to defeat and ultimately destroy a life. Doubts, confusion, despair, and loneliness are tactics he uses to whirl us around and knock us down unguarded. Watch for him to arrive just in time to hurt you at the worst possible moment and when your life couldn't seem to get worse.

Satan's the father of lies and will try to deceive you through others close to you. He'll come in like a firing squad and seek to destroy your goodness, your hope, your faith, thus halting your perseverance. And he won't stop until he's tried to destroy everything and everyone dear to you.

Satan wants you to feel bad about yourself, to feel unworthy of someone's love. He'll try to convince you that if your own parents wouldn't stand by you, then no one else will love you either. But that's not true.

If Satan can keep you from the truth, he can keep you in the dark and strip you of peace, hope, and love. You have the power, through the blood of Jesus Christ, to stop Satan from taking you down in the devastating rubble of your broken home. Refuse to sit in the dark, pull back the drapes, and let God's light in, banishing Satan from all corners of your life.

Latch onto God and don't let go. Allow His light to lead you out of Satan's devices. Be determined that no force can or will stop you as long as God's on your side.

In this world there will be losses and disappointments that you have no control over, you've already seen that. But with God, there's a way out of every trouble and an ultimate plan to take you to a better world, Heaven, where nothing evil will touch. God is love and He's your Father of lights; He never changes!

Every good thing given and every perfect gift is from above, coming down from the Father of lights, with whom there is no variation or shifting shadow.
—James 1:17

Fill your paper with the breathings of your heart.
– William Wordsworth

Does Jesus Care?

Does Jesus care when I've said "goodbye"
to the dearest on earth to me,
and my sad heart aches till it nearly breaks,
is it aught to Him? Does He see?
—Frank E. Graeff

Sometimes we not only lose our parents when we're placed in foster care or a children's home; we can also lose our siblings. My baby brother never lived with me again after the initial breakup of our former family. I discovered, while at school, that he had been adopted into the family of one of my classmates. I was happy to find he was loved and safe, but my heart was breaking as I tried to hide my tears.

In addition to my brother's adoption, another sibling was also adopted. Wednesday's Child, an adoption network through the local media, told my little sister's story in hopes a permanent home would be found. The song, *All You Need is Love* by the Beatles, played on the local TV station while our little sister was featured as the Valentine Wednesday's Child. My brother and I watched tearfully as she and the news lady baked cookies on the set. It was bad enough to live without our parents, whom we deeply loved and needed, but then to be forced to live without another sibling was most cruel and unfair.

I've found since the adoption of my baby brother that he never remembered me or the time we shared together as a family. He did express he had felt loved by the people who adopted him.

You may also find death can sever blood ties as was the case with my older brother who joined me later in a foster home. We were teenagers when he died suddenly and unexpectedly in the home we shared with two other siblings. I recall the nightmare and the decision my parents made in removing him from life support.

I was the older girl in my family and never forgot or stopped loving my siblings for one moment. I was determined to build our relationship from where we picked up later. Perhaps you, too, have suffered a fragment in the bonds with your siblings. You may find as I did, sometimes those family ties are never the same after they are broken in childhood.

All of us have realities in our lives we wish we could change, but the simple fact is, we cannot go back and alter the events of our history. We can only choose to move forward, making new memories with stronger connections. We can use our tragedies to help us love deeper and cherish the time we have with those who come into our lives.

Oh, yes, He cares, I know He cares,
His heart is touched with my grief;
When the days are weary, the long nights dreary,
I know my Savior cares.
—Frank E. Graeff

Fill your paper with the breathings of your heart.
—William Wordsworth

Our Pet Friends

Your soft breath has left me with
God's beating heart
and that's how it'll always be—
I'll live in you, you'll live in me.

Some of us not only lose our parents and siblings when we are placed in foster care or in an orphanage, we also lose our pets. For many of us, our pets were the only friends we had in our former home. They were our loyal, attentive friends who were there when we needed someone to love and accept us.

I had several animal friends in my youth. Two dogs and a kitten were among my most memorable pets. Before I was taken from my family, I befriended a kitten who lived in the stairwell of the apartment where I resided. Every night when all the neighbors were sleeping, I tiptoed out into the hallway and played with the kitten, dangling a string over his head and watching him try to catch it. The kitten helped me feel better by soothing away some of the sadness I was experiencing. The bond we shared helped my loneliness.

The first few months following the breakup of my family I was overwhelmed in devastating sorrow, not only missing my family, but my animals too. Our pets are larger than life, especially when we are young. We can find ourselves feeling that everything we once held dear has been taken from us. And in many respects, that may be true.

There are many opinions on the belief that animals will be in Heaven with the saved. Whether they are or not, I take great comfort in believing I'll see my pets again. I can't prove it definitively, but I believe it's possible. As long as the idea of this brings comfort to me and I hold it only as an opinion, I see no harm in accepting it as truth for myself.

Perhaps you've said goodbye to everyone dear to you, including your pets. I found it helps to keep their memories alive and with you. This may be an excellent time to use your extra page as a place to draw a sketch of your beloved family and include your pet in the drawing. If you have a talent for creating abstract art, you could design a page showcasing all of the feelings and emotions your pet has brought to your life. Establishing a memorial of those we love can be a beautiful way to find solace and acceptance of our pet loss.

You may also consider volunteering at your local animal shelter. Having a place to share your affection for animals may be a wonderful way to honor your former pet. In addition, if your foster parents permit, perhaps you could adopt or foster an animal. There are many opportunities in today's world for nurturing and caring for animals. It's possible another animal is waiting for a home too!

In the Bible, we find God has respect for His created beings. Proverbs 12:10 reads: *A righteous man has regard for the life of his animal.* Loving and caring for an animal is a wonderful attribute in the eyes of the Lord!

When an animal touches our lives
with their soft breath,
they give us a portion of God's heart
and leave us with a piece of Heaven.

Fill your paper with the breathings of your heart.
—William Wordsworth

Determination

*It's on the strength of observation and reflection
that one finds a way.
So we must dig and delve unceasingly.*
—Claude Monet

Be determined that better days are coming for you! It can be easy to sink into gloom and despair when feelings of abandonment erupt in your heart. And who could blame you, your life has been turned upside down. Dwelling excessively on your disappointments won't help you in the long run. Experiencing your pain is welcomed as an avenue to healing, but remaining in the pain can only prolong suffering.

It's important to be easy on yourself as you recover from trauma. Some have found it helpful to take on the hardest tasks at the beginning of their day and then wind down with more gentle goals. Perhaps you would want to keep a daily diary of your accomplishments. It can be very rewarding, especially on discouraging days, to look back on all that you've accomplished.

Walks are a peaceful way to settle your mind and refocus. Perhaps ask a friend to walk with you so that you are safe and take the time to reset your determination. Having a strong will is one of the attributes of survivors. Decide you're going to be one of them and shape your activities around being an over comer. With God's help, you can overcome the most dreadful events!

My sun sets to rise again.
—Elizabeth Barrett Browning

Fill your paper with the breathings of your heart.
–William Wordsworth

Confusion & Despair

Do not be anxious about anything, but in everything
by prayer and supplication with thanksgiving
let your requests be made known to God.
—Philippians 4:6

It's normal to experience a spectrum of emotions when trying to survive loss and coping with new circumstances. Don't be afraid when these moments come; they come to all of us at some point in our lives. What's important is how we approach them and what we do with the raw emotions.

There will be times when confusion, coupled with feelings of despair, will overwhelm you. No one can take the confusion or suffering from you, but there is a technique that has helped me make it through difficult nights. Perhaps it will help you.

Imagine God holding your hand as you weep. There's great power in using your imagination. Just as reading a book or watching a movie can transport you to another place and time, so can what you focus on and allow your mind to think on.

Thoughts are powerful. I like to think of them as time travelers for the mind, where I can weave in and out of different worlds within moments. And so it can be with your troubles; they don't have to pin you down or force you to stay in the world of doom and gloom.

Use your mind to calm yourself on your pillow. Before closing your teary eyes for sleep, open your Bible and start reading from the book of Psalms. Prayer with imagery can go a long way to helping you wake up to the promise of brighter days peeking over the new horizons.

The Lord bless you, and keep you;
The Lord make His face shine on you,
and be gracious to you;
The Lord lift up His countenance on you,
and give you peace.
—Numbers 6:24-26

Fill your paper with the breathings of your heart.
–William Wordsworth

Hidden Talent

*"Great things are done by
a series of small things
brought together."*
−Vincent Van Gogh

One of the best remedies for a bad day is to do something kind for someone else. Perhaps write a note or send an email or text of encouragement to someone else.

When I was a foster child−discouraged, sad, moping around about my losses−I was advised to learn the art of cooking, specifically baking cakes. I can recall baking a lot of cakes for my foster family and for my siblings! There was value in staying busy and productive during my pain. The losses still followed me to the mixing bowl, but they did not defeat me.

As a result of starting so young at baking cakes, I grew to enjoy creating festive dishes. I even enrolled in classes while in high school and college so that I could aspire to greater culinary skills. A few years ago I was hired as a personal chef for two of my friends. Is it possible God was allowing me to discover hidden talents so that I could take care of myself while helping others?

Perhaps you are drawn to a musical instrument, or desire to make a difference in the world. Ask God to reveal your talents and He'll allow those to be known to you. Look for the answers to come in many possible ways, perhaps through the suggestion of your new parents or through the dreams and desires of your heart.

Fill your paper with the breathings of your heart.
-William Wordsworth

Gift of Time

Neither can the wave that has passed by be recalled,
nor the hour which has passed return again.
—Ovid

When we are first hit with a significant loss or life-altering event, our initial response is usually that of shock and confusion. Later we may experience disbelief, despair, anger, rage, and even depression. The mind must be allowed time to sort out these feelings and adjust.

Change has a way of making us better or worse. Some of us may go to extremes in finding ways to cope. It's difficult to come to terms with our tormented emotions. Instead of allowing time for the situation to get better sometimes we step in and try to fix it ourselves. In doing so, we may make matters worse due to lack of experience and maturity to deal with it effectively. It's imperative we take positive actions toward the things we can change and leave the rest for God to handle.

Time can be a wonderful friend when we are in transitional phases of suffering. Trials, sorrows, and disappointments can be catalysts for personal growth, new opportunities, and a greater sense of personal awareness. I've found that when significant events happen in our lives, we often emerge a different person than we were before. The gift of time is a friend that can re-frame our perspective, leading us to the well of wisdom, healing, and self-discovery.

Fill your paper with the breathings of your heart.
—William Wordsworth

Skies Filled With Smiles

The leaves of memory
seemed to make
a mournful rustling in the dark.
—Longfellow

Invariably, you will have flashbacks to your former life; some will make you smile as you cherish their memory, and others will cause a flood of tears. This is the mind's way of trying to cope as your spirit seeks harmony during the upheaval and chaos.

When these moments come upon you, they can be like a storm, leaving you shaken, unsteady, emotional, scared, confused, and drained with fatigue. Reach out for God's hand and you won't go through it alone.

Close your eyes and ask God to take your mind to a peaceful place; He's already there anyway, with open arms, waiting for you. Imagine walking hand in hand with Him along a sandy beach or serenading you with the moon's halo illuminating over you.

Create a place in your mind that makes you feel happy, a scene with events that help to redirect your painful memories taking you to new dreams and ambitions. Imagine God's face as a tender Father trying to comfort and make you happy. He is your refuge where comfort and peace is found; He will carry you through. Run into His arms as His child and let your beautiful imagination take you to rivers of joy and skies filled with smiles.

God inspires us to smile
from the inside out.

Fill your paper with the breathings of your heart.
– William Wordsworth

Every Breath is a Gift

Do not delay; the golden memories fly!
—Longfellow

It's not easy waking up each day and finding we are still in a children's home or residing in foster care. Sadly, our lives rarely just snap back into place. We can be tempted to wish for things to be better and fail to celebrate every moment of our lives.

I can recall wishing for my eighteenth birthday to arrive so that I could find my parents, gather my siblings around me, and be a family once again. In wishing for years to pass, we may find at the end of the wait, we wasted our lives and never lived or enjoyed the moments and years before.

The regret from wishing one's life away is often a far greater price than we'd want to pay in the end. Many on their death beds have often expressed they wished they had spent more time living in the present. And while it's healthy to hope and make plans for the future, we must guard our heart from worse sorrow later because we were waiting for a day to make us happy.

The book of Ecclesiastes is a powerful book on the brevity of life. Ecclesiastes 3:11 reads: *He has made everything beautiful in its time. Also, He has put eternity into man's heart, yet so that he cannot find out what God has done from the beginning to the end.* Eternity is so deeply rooted within our heart, we cannot fathom all the workings of God. So we must trust Him, and not try to figure out everything or make decisions based upon perceived future events. God is the Alpha and the Omega, in other words, the beginning and the end of all things concerning us. We must place our lives in His hands and allow Him, as our sculptor, to transform our lives into His unique beauty and design.

In a moment, what we have could be taken away. If you're reading this book you probably understand that better than most. Life is precious and every breath we take is a gift; let's use it wisely, letting God have the things we can't change while accepting the beauty and wonder of each new day.

Fill your paper with the breathings of your heart.
−William Wordsworth

Bridge of Hope

ook for God's plans and purposes for your life to show up in the wounds you've suffered. Survivors are the bridges for others to find hope and healing during great suffering. Even though you can't change your circumstances, you can change how you view them.

Have you considered that perhaps some day when your burdens have been lifted, someone else may need the wisdom you've gained out of painful experiences? Is it not possible God knew you'd make it to the other side of the pain so that you could become someone's champion?

God is the key to a new life. He longs to love, bless, and soothe away your tears and He uses His people to bring about those plans. If you turn to Him and love Him, He will make a new path, bringing new friends and family who will love and cherish you. Doors of opportunity will also open. Reach out to other believers, sharing your burdens. In doing so, you will allow God's family to help you walk across bridges of hope as the turbulent waters beneath dissipate.

Count it a beautiful thing to fall into the all-encompassing arms of God. He will use your strength and beauty to help another. Not only will He help others through you, but He'll transport you to a new season in your life. He doesn't promise you won't have new challenges, but He does promise to unfold new connections and aspirations as He rebuilds your heart with joy and wisdom.

On earth you will have troubles, but with God, you are promised deliverance from every one of them. Be confident that as you place your trust in God, all sorrows will be ebbed away on the shores of Heaven.

We rejoice in our sufferings,
knowing that suffering produces endurance.
–Romans 5:3

Fill your paper with the breathings of your heart.
– William Wordsworth

Be a Friend

Oh the trip is shorter when you've got a friend;
Gotta find that rainbow beyond the bend.
—Elvis Presley

When the past comes back to hurt you, go ahead and cry—it's healthy to release sorrow —and then find something productive to do. Perhaps visit a lonely neighbor and offer to help them in some way. Sometimes people just want to talk with someone, a trusted confidant who'll listen to their troubles. In listening to someone else, you may be surprised at how much better you feel about your problems. It's also possible they have valuable wisdom you could benefit from. Friendships come in all sizes and ages; don't be afraid to reach out to someone wiser and older than yourself.

Consider befriending an outcast where you go to school. We're all valuable because we're made in God's image. Perhaps your broken wing, joined with theirs, could create two soaring eagles who one day will fly as two because they gleaned strength from the other.

You also may consider reading to the blind or if you know a blind person, be their eyes to the beauty of our world. Perhaps arrange a visit with them in their yard and sit describing the birds, trees, butterflies, and the sky. Or gather a bouquet of wild flowers and present it to them and then describe the floral beauty. In spending time with someone who is blind you are inspiring a luminous bond of friendship.

Personal connections can inspire hope and is another benefit of extending ourselves to others during times of pain. Friends are able to see the good in us, perhaps qualities we never knew were there. God uses all circumstances for the plans and purposes of His creation. Often we can feel a deep sense of satisfaction at the end of a day that has been spent inspiring a new dream or helping another.

Something very powerful happens when we help others: tears cease falling as our burdens lighten. Often new friendships are formed through the common bonds of suffering. Friends have a way of softening the sorrows of life and mending the tears in our souls.

There may be someone who needs your compassionate heart to glean understanding from. You can be a well of strength for others who may suffer like you in the future. Consider stretching out your weary hand to someone else who may need your compassionate heart. Be exceptional in kindness and compassion. Life is wonderful when kindred hearts assemble together in the beauty of friendship.

How far that little candle throws his beams!
So shines a good deed in a weary world.
—William Shakespeare

Fill your paper with the breathings of your heart.
-William Wordsworth

Anger

Be still and know that I am God.
—Psalm 46:10

It's normal to get angry and want to lash out at someone when we're hurting. Having discretion, however, will save us from compounding our problems. While there is healthy anger, specifically when injustices occur, anger that's allowed to simmer overnight could result in rage or even violent outbursts. At the least, it can impair one's health. If we learn early to temper our emotions, it will become second nature to control unsavory feelings as we grow older.

Getting still with God will allow us time to work out powerful emotions and help prevent us from doing something we could regret later. It's alright to share all of your feelings with the Lord. He's available at all hours of the day and night, just waiting for your call. He won't hang up on you or tire from hearing your troubles again and again. He's also the greatest secret keeper there is!

Instead of lashing out in anger, use its fire to light a worthwhile purpose such as a cause dear to your heart. Consider being a volunteer at a shelter or soup kitchen for the homeless. Supporting a worthy cause is a great place to allow the embers of anger to burn away feelings of hostility.

God desires to help you with whatever troubles you, so tell Him why you're angry and plead for His help. He already knows it anyway, but sharing yourself–scars, flaws, insecurities, and angered emotions–help to form a bond between you and your forever Father. A bond formed with your Father in Heaven is unbreakable; no force of nature or act of mankind can take it from you, ever!

Be angry, and do not sin;
ponder in your own hearts on your beds,
and be silent. Selah
–Psalm 4:4

Fill your paper with the breathings of your heart.
– William Wordsworth

Be Someone's Smile

They that sow in tears shall reap in joy.
—Psalm 126:5

We can all find ourselves in harsh places at times with no way to change the circumstances. But there is something we can do while we wait for the sad times to pass: we can choose to honor God and others with our time and talents.

Often we are called to make the greatest sacrifice for others when we feel least able to do so. Putting our worries aside and allowing the tears to continue flowing while doing good is what it means to sow seeds while in tears.

When you feel like staying in bed with the covers pulled over you head, why not get up, get dressed, and spend the day trying to be someone's smile? If you can't go anywhere, you could get the address of a children's hospital and pen notes or create picture art for the children who may have long term illnesses.

If you strive to help others who are also sad and dealing with difficult circumstances, you not only encourage them, but you also encourage yourself. At the end of the day, you will feel happier for helping someone else while your own troubles were momentarily out of your mind. And you never know what blessings and joy await later when God brings your works to fruition with a new season. We cannot know how God will turn our tears into blessings, but we can be assured He promises to do so with laughter and joy.

Fill your paper with the breathings of your heart.
–William Wordsworth

You Are Beloved

Behold, we count them happy which endure.
Ye have heard of the patience of Job,
and have seen the end of the Lord;
that the Lord is very pitiful, and of tender mercy.
—James 5:11

Like Job, if you continue to endure suffering while maintaining integrity in your heart, the Lord will also bless you with compassion and mercy. We may not know how we'll reach a new horizon, but it is certain we will as long as we keep our focus on the One who created us.

The Lord cherishes you deeply and has seen every tear you've cried, and He knows who has hurt you. He has also noticed when you've had courage and done the right thing in spite of the pressures of life and temptations.

We also learn from the story of Job that he had friends who tied to be helpful, but at times blamed him for his bad circumstances implying he had done something to deserve God's wrath. It's usually best if we say very little when our friends are suffering. Job's friends did that in the beginning, but later gave advice and wisdom that was not always correct despite the compassion and love they had for him. We find in the end of Job's suffering, it was God who had the final word in his life!

It's important we view ourselves and circumstances through the lens of God before we leap to conclusions as to why we are beset with trials, disappointments, and losses. The Lord knows how strong you've been and all the hardships you've endured. He is with you at every stage of your life, the highs and the lows. His presence is permanent, but your troubles are not. Like the changing seasons, this season of suffering will end. Trust God and strive for His wisdom and spiritual excellence.

Fill your paper with the breathings of your heart.
–William Wordsworth

Open Your Heart

After being hurt we can begin to close our heart off from receiving and giving love, essentially pulling down the blinds of our hearts and refusing to let anyone in. But this is not how God wants us to live our life nor is it best for us. He never intended for any of us to shut ourselves away from the love and care of others. In doing so, we could be nullifying God's plan for creating a new home and family.

Suffering produces strength and self control produces nobility. Some of the most noble people I've known have had a past whose lives were filled with tragedy. Pain and loss often form the deepest and most meaningful bonds of love and friendship. When I reflect upon those dearest to me, and the ones who have had the greatest impact in my life, it has been shared tragedy that made the difference.

Allow your heart to be open to others who may not be your blood family. Many children have risen out of the despairing wounds of family loss and found a loving home with people who were not their biological family. It's okay to reserve a special place in your heart for your biological family, but it's equally right and good to allow room for others to love you. Take God's hand and let hope blossom a new tomorrow.

Fill your paper with the breathings of your heart.
—William Wordsworth

Bubbling With Hope

When we are living in a children's home or in a foster home, we can begin to worry that our lives will never be happy again. As each day passes and we wake to yet another day without our parents, we can begin to despair and lose hope. Hopelessness can have a detrimental affect on our spirit. God knew this before we ever felt hopeless. Proverbs 13:12 reads: *Hope deferred makes the heart sick, But desire fulfilled is a tree of life.* Be assured, however, God has not called any of us to be hopeless and despair from the wounds of life. The Bible is full of Scriptures concerning hope. God's Word is a place where we can replenish hope when we find ourselves on the verge of despair.

Romans 15:13 reads: *Now the God of hope fill you with all joy and peace in believing, that ye may abound in hope, through the power of the Holy Ghost.* This verse is confirmation that God is the source of our hope. Not only is He the way in which we can obtain it, but He paints the picture of hope overflowing. No human can provide this kind of hope; it's not earthly. It comes from the spiritual realm and is provided by the Holy Spirit.

The next time you find yourself needing a good dose of hope, read this wonderful Scripture as you pray for God's hope to wash over your troubled spirit. With God as your hope, you can expect a beautiful future to unfold in His providential care.

The well of Providence is deep;
it's the buckets we bring to it that are small.
—Mary Webb

Fill your paper with the breathings of your heart.
– William Wordsworth

Prayer Letters

God longs to spend time with you so that He can inspire, love, encourage, and lift you with hope. We can spend time with God in many ways: reading His word, worshiping Him with thanksgiving, songs, and prayer.

Have you considered writing your prayers to God in a journal? There were times in my life when I found just sitting down with my favorite notebook and a pen were wonderful ways to help me settle or strengthen me during the trials and sorrows in my life. I found later that some of my prayers had been answered, and often in ways I could not have imagined.

Along with my prayers, I also penned favorite poems, quotes, and other significant events that happened in my life. Later, I saw how God had been listening and working things out for my good.

Consider keeping a journal of your dreams, desires, and your prayers and you may find, as I have, that there was a Savior there all along, taking notice of you and all things concerning you. Soon, you will find God's affirmations showing up on the pages when you see a pattern of His care and love for you unfolding.

Fill your paper with the breathings of your heart.
– William Wordsworth

Tear-Shaped Heart

*Suppressed grief suffocates, it rages within the breast,
and is forced to multiply its strength.*
—Ovid

It's not unusual for many foster children to be shifted from home to home before leaving the system. I lived in six different homes before becoming an adult and living on my own.

When sorrow and upheaval occur one on top of the other before we've had time to recover from the previous sorrow, this can create what I term a tear-shaped heart. Anyone who suffers extensively for prolonged periods of time can also develop a weeping spirit.

I discovered one day, when some things had greatly upset me, that I had a been conditioned to have a spirit of sorrow. I knew I had to take steps to find joy and focus on being hopeful rather than allowing every disappointment to freeze my heart into a tear drop.

It's not easy to take our thoughts captive, but it is possible. Praying, meditating on comforting Scriptures and focusing on other personal victories can give us the strength to allow God to heal our weeping hearts.

He gives us people to help, but ultimately it's God who heals and makes one whole.

The next time you feel consumed with sorrow, try to shift your mind to a memory that made you smile and then meditate on that happy memory while smiling through the tears. It's a known fact that the act of smiling tricks the brain into thinking it's happy. The brain doesn't sort out why you're happy; it simply accepts the smile as being happy. Smiling is also known to reduce stress, lower blood pressure, increase longevity, and help the heart.

Fill your paper with the breathings of your heart.
–William Wordsworth

The Lord's Presence

One day, I was working in my flower garden and a small, blue butterfly landed on the top of my hand. Enchanted by the tiny creature, I took notice of her, giggled with delight and thanked God for the creature's marvelous appearing. I proceeded to work in my flowers, moving my hand around as I continued with my gardening, but the tiny butterfly did not fly away or remove herself from my hand.

The butterfly eventually flew away, only to return to my arm for a while. I was quite amused by the fact that she stayed near me the entire time I spent in my garden. Is it not possible God whispered to the butterfly to grace her presence near me as a reminder of the Lord's gentle presence? I've had many events like this occur. I like to think that God has left rose petals for me to find.

The next time you feel anxious, visit a garden or park and let God's spirit fill you with the wonder and tranquility of nature. In the stillness, you'll experience God's beautiful, intricate world.

Fill your paper with the breathings of your heart.
—William Wordsworth

God's Poetic Heart

When I'm walking in nature, I often think of the following Scripture and a million little worlds begin to open up: *For ye shall go out with joy, and be led forth with peace: the mountains and the hills shall break forth before you into singing, and all the trees of the field shall clap their hands.* —Isaiah 55:12

I've heard the whisper of God echoing softly like a ripple on the ocean and I believe you have too. God's creation unfolds many times like a marvelous play. When you see a butterfly fluttering near you on a sunny day or a cardinal peering in your direction, you can be assured your Father in Heaven has allowed you to embrace His eternal beauty.

The Bible is full of the poetic side of God's heart. God is the master of poetry as evidenced in the books of poetry, especially Song of Songs, Psalms, and Proverbs.

Writing poetry or short stories can be very good therapy for a broken spirit. Even if you do not publish your expressions, getting your thoughts on paper can help you unwind and calm your mind for a better night's rest. Perhaps you could pen a few thoughts on your extra page; you may be surprised how much better you feel for getting your raw feelings onto print.

Fill your paper with the breathings of your heart.
–William Wordsworth

You Have a Future

*"For I know the thoughts that I think toward you, says
the LORD, thoughts of peace and not of evil, to give
you a future and a hope."*
—Jeremiah 29:11

Many years ago I fell in love with this Scripture and the comforting reassurance it held. After losing your family, you can begin to feel unimportant, wondering if God even cares what's happened to you. Be assured, He does and is working behind the scenes on your current problems to orchestrate your future.

God's definition of your future may not line up with your views or what others believe for you. He doesn't promise you won't suffer again, and that you will be granted a future with fancy earthly possessions lavished on you. But the future you can depend on with God is one filled with peace, love, security, and the promise of an eternal relationship with Him.

It can take time for the broken pieces to fall into place. As you go through life and its trials come against you, don't put trust in what you see in the physical realm. Instead, put your trust in the promise that God is preparing His absolute best for you. Mathew 7:11 reads: *If you then, being evil, know how to give good gifts to your children, how much more will your Father who is in heaven give what is good to those who ask Him!* We find from this Scripture that no earthly parent can rival God's gifts for His children!

Your story isn't finished yet; God promises that a better time awaits you. As you walk through the rain of earthly sorrows, keep hoping with expectation that God's plans, purposes, and blessings will unfold as each chapter of your life is lived.

Fill your paper with the breathings of your heart.
–William Wordsworth

Silver Linings

And we know that in all things
God works for the good
of those who love Him,
who have been called
according to His purpose.
—Romans 8:28

There's tremendous encouragement to be found in the above Scripture. Essentially, God has promised that all things, both good and bad, will work out for the good of those who love Him and obey Him.

We all make mistakes and wish we had a chance to make a different decision. We can even brutalize ourselves further by dwelling on it and punishing ourselves. God does not want us to do this. He pleads for us to let go of the burdens that weigh us down.

God doesn't remember our sins once we've repented of them. Hebrews 8:12 reads: *For I will be merciful toward their iniquities, and I will remember their sins no more.* Another passage of Scripture that affirms God doesn't hold our sins against us is found in Psalm 103:12. It reads: As *far as the east is from the west, so far does he remove our transgressions from us.*

Our sins are so removed that they cannot affect us any more. We are safe from all condemnation for our sins, as if they had not been committed at all.

If God doesn't hold our offenses against us or remember them once they're forgiven, why should we? We must forgive ourselves and move forward with wisdom we've gained from the experiences. It's essential that we live for God and place our lives in His hands. In doing so, we are guaranteed that God will guide and direct our paths.

When life's trials and storms begin to beat down on you, remind yourself of God's promise. Hold to Him as a beacon of light, knowing that even as you suffer, He is taking the pieces from the wreckage and turning them into His providential care of you.

Behind the dark curtain of despair,
pain and suffering are painting a silver lining.

Fill your paper with the breathings of your heart.
–William Wordsworth

Treasures

Ecclesiastes 7:2 reads: *It is better to go to a house of mourning than to go to a house of feasting, because that is the end of every man, and the living takes it to heart.* To some this may seem so contrary to living a joyful life when we're told attending a funeral is better for us than going to a celebration. Does this Scripture imply that we are to reside in a state of grief at all times? No, it does not.

If we study this Scripture further, we find that sorrow allows us an opportunity to do some serious soul searching and deep reflection on our own mortality. We also tend to focus on leaving a legacy worth remembering after we're gone. Whereas when we attend a party, we tend to lavish ourselves with scrumptious food and activities not really thinking seriously about our soul and if we're ready for eternity.

Most of us know first-hand how it feels to be abandoned and betrayed; we know all too well the heart-wrenching tears of being children without a family or a place to belong. What do we do with all the bad experiences, wounds, and disappointments we've been left with? We can use them as insight when trying to find meaning for our suffering.

Some day you may have a home of your own with children to raise. I can speak from experience that it can be scary finding you may soon be a parent and worry you won't know how to do it well because you never had a role model.

If you're fearful of becoming a parent try digging through your old emotional baggage and discarding all the bad stuff while keeping the wisdom you're gained. Reflect upon how you felt when someone didn't have time for you and decide you'll be there for your child. If a parent didn't give up a negative lifestyle, such as alcoholism, be determined you won't allow any substance to prevent you from being a well-adjusted parent.

Deep love, respect, and empathy are the God-given attributes that are born out of life-altering events. If we examine the bags of our past, we can find many treasures to keep and plenty to discard. Make the decision that you won't repeat what was done to you and choose to use its insight to teach you a better way.

Fill your paper with the breathings of your heart.
—William Wordsworth

God's Heir

When I was a foster child I grieved not having fully belonged to someone. This is a normal reaction to being a foster child or an orphan. Ephesians 1:4 reads: *Just as He chose us in Him before the foundation of the world, that we would be holy and blameless before Him.* God made a plan for you to belong before the world was created!

Our value is further enhanced in knowing we were not an afterthought: God was intentional when He created us to be a part of His everlasting plans. We are permanent with Him, through Him, and in Him as we follow His ways.

Romans 8:17 tells us we are not only God's children, but we are also His heir with His son Jesus. You not only belong, but you have an inheritance with God your Father. This knowledge is central to help smooth away some of the painful feelings of rejection.

The next time you question if you belong, remind yourself that God has willed His entire heart and estate to you. A treasure trove awaits you in Heaven!

Fill your paper with the breathings of your heart.
–William Wordsworth

Tears Into Pearls

You have kept count of my tossings;
put my tears in your bottle.
Are they not in your book?
—Psalm 56:8

We learn from the above Scripture that God takes notice of each tear you cry; He collects each one and keeps them in His bottle. God's aware of how you suffer even when you cannot see Him or feel Him near. He's been there all along holding you close to His breast. When you feel alone or forgotten, remember God knows every hurt; His heart is saturated with empathy for you.

One day, God will take all of your tears and make you into a beautiful strand of pearls. So the next time you see a tear fall down your cheek, smile and know God's designing you into a rare and beautiful jewel. On the following page are lyrics I wrote for you. You are not alone; I give you my lyrical hand to hold.

Tears Into Pearls

Verse One
    when you're forsaken, feeling small
    left breaking inside
    God whispers, I'll stay
    you're the apple of my eye
Verse Two
    when all of your walls have fallen down
    you're left in pieces
    He's your living stone
    to rebuild everything on
Verse Three
    when you've hurt yourself and everyone else
    can't find a way out
    or make it right
    hold onto Jesus, He's your light
Verse Four
    God knows what you've been through and who's hurt you
    He will heal you whole
    He's your morning star
    all of your tears are in His jar
Bridge
    He sees you on your knees
    He grieves too, pleads,
    let go of the burden weighing you down
    embrace my light, you belong with me now
    you belong with me now
Chorus
    I will turn all your tears into pearls
    create a lovely strand
    when each tear falls
    in the hollow of my hand.

Fill your paper with the breathings of your heart.
— William Wordsworth

God's Pen

God uses tragedy to build greatness within us. Give Him your sorrows, disappointments, and fears and He will transform you into a beautiful woman of strength and character. With God's pen in your hand, you can choose to be the protagonist of your own story: no matter what the other characters do or what events unfold, you can choose to embrace hope, love, forgiveness, and compassion.

The great sacrifice Christ made on the cross has left us a blueprint of Heaven and an indelible impression on our souls. Keep holding onto good people and living honorably and you will have a rewarding future. The Lord cups your tear-stained face in His nail-scarred hands; He will collect every tear you cry and give you a beautiful forever.

Upon completing this book, I whispered prayer over you. I am with you in spirit and love today, sharing in your wounds and celebrating your triumphs! Together we can be change agents for a better world!

Your friend,
Teresa Ann Winton

Fill your paper with the breathings of your heart.
–William Wordsworth

About the Author

Raised in Kentucky and taken from her parents at age eight, Teresa Ann Winton was placed in foster care for the duration of her childhood until she went to Florida College. She continued her education at Western Kentucky University where she studied early childhood education. Teresa has also studied fashion tailoring, interior design, ballet, nutrition, and homeopathic medicines.

Her first published book, *Pieces of the Pearl*, chronicles her life as a foster child, where she gives a candid view into her life as a vulnerable and abandoned child. In spite of the abuse, poverty, and neglect, she persevered through the devastation, refusing to succumb to despair.

Teresa has used her past as insight to help inspire and encourage others who have survived backgrounds similar to her own. She has counseled and helped several teen girls, specifically becoming an appointed mentor for one of those she has helped.

Additionally, Teresa has also published *Tears in the Lilies, Two Tears of a Heart, Impressions of Eternal Love, The King's Son,* poetry at Crossway Publications, and song lyrics.

CPSIA information can be obtained
at www.ICGtesting.com
Printed in the USA
LVHW051251231220
674969LV00004B/647